T0129838

Couple Minutes
of
Your Time

MARLON & LISA MARSHALL

authorHOUSE®

AuthorHouse™
1663 Liberty Drive
Bloomington, IN 47403
www.authorhouse.com
Phone: 1 (800) 839-8640

Published by AuthorHouse 02/28/2019

ISBN: 978-1-5462-7366-0 (sc)
ISBN: 978-1-5462-7365-3 (e)

Print information available on the last page.

Any people depicted in stock imagery provided by Getty Images are models,
and such images are being used for illustrative purposes only.
Certain stock imagery © Getty Images.

This book is printed on acid-free paper.

Inspiration

Remember when you make yourself available to God, he will use you. Are you making yourself available for his use or the use of the world? Attitude is everything!!! NotPerfectButWorthIt!!! Stay Blessed!!!

Remember make a point this day to lift your voice and greatly extol our LORD, for when people gather together to praise him our perspectives change, our heavy load diminishes, our sorrow decreases and joy comes alive. No matter what your circumstances, may this day be a day of renewal and refreshing from the presence of the LORD. Attitude is everything!!! NotPerfectButWorthIt!!! Stay Blessed!!!

Remember the good you do today, people will often forget tomorrow. Do good anyway... Because God sees everything, and will bless you accordingly... Attitude is everything!!! NotPerfectButWorthIt!!! Stay Blessed!!!

Remember asking God to bless you is a wonderful thing, but asking God to use the Blessing he gave you to be a Blessing to others is stepping up your Christianity to the next level... Attitude is everything!! NotPerfectButWorthIt!!! Stay Blessed!!!

Remember allow God's Blessing to flow through you.... Attitude is everything!! NotPerfectButWorthIt!!! Stay Blessed!!!

Remember God's give us the "Free Will" to do absolutely whatever we choose to. Just think about it; we have the freedom to do anything we want in our "Will." Oh....but don't expect God to honor our "Free Will" choices; it doesn't matter how you justify your "Free Will" choices.... God is only required to honor our "God Will" choices. If you are unaware were to locate "God's Will" for your life.... Allow me to direct you to the most famous book; it remains on the best seller list each year... "The BIBLE!" What "Will" will you choose "Free" or "God's!"

Attitude is everything!! NotPerfectButWorthIt!!! Stay Blessed!!!

Remember I'm blessed; two simple words, but often not said without any true consideration of the meaning. When asked how I am doing... I say "I'm Blessed", but really I am either annoyed, upset, frustrated, or on those rare times... I actually feel "Blessed." Well, as I woke up this morning, and I thought about those two simple words... I started thinking... I'm Blessed because, I have the abilities of my mind and body, my family does as well, I have the ability to be a servant of God.... so I'm Blessed! Being blessed doesn't mean that "Life" is fair and will always be easy, but being blessed recognizes despite "Life" God has given you undeserving "Favor....!" So the next time someone ask you "How are you doing"; say "I'm Blessed" loud and proud... because in reality you really are... Attitude is everything!!! NotPerfectButWorthIt!!! Stay Blessed!!!

Remember relationship or religion; only you can decide for yourself how it will be with God. It's a "Relationship" that God seeks to have. Attitude is everything!!! NotPerfectButWorthIt!!! Stay Blessed!!!

Remember if you are tired of reaping the same old seed that is not "Blessing" you or others than try sowing some seed that will "Bless" you and others. You reap what you sow!!! Attitude is everything!!! NotPerfectButWorthIt!!! Stay Blessed!!!

Remember "Keep your PEACE so you can keep your POWER." The Devil waits for opportunities to STEAL, KILL, and DESTORY your PEACE and gain his POWER over you... so...Keep the 2 P's - PEACE and POWER! Attitude is everything!!! NotPerfectButWorthIt!!! Stay Blessed!!!

Remember that God's Blessing only reaches those in need through other's like ourselves....Make yourself available for the flow of God to reach others....and watch the flow of God move through you, the next person, and on and on and on....Watching God at work; it's nothing like it!!!! Attitude is everything!!! NotPerfectButWorthIt!!! Stay Blessed!!!

Remember If God has placed something deep into your spirit for you to "ACT" on; what the problem be...??? Oh... I get it....; you're scare and afraid that you may "FAIL"... It's a valid thought and emotion...Again, my question is "What are you waiting for? Sometimes we can be our own worst enemy; trust in the word of God, and what he's put in you. Now get up, and get to moving on your "PROMISE" from

God. Attitude is everything!!! NotPerfectButWorthIt!!! Stay Blessed!!!

Remember When we started dating our significant other we immediately gave them trust and surrendered ourselves to them and them alone. We started to believe in them and follow them... without reservation. We got to know about them and they did the same with us...However, the one that knew us before we knew ourselves we reserve our trust and we hesitate on surrendering to him... hmmmm? Let's activate our FAITH, put our trust in drive, surrender in first or second gear, and OBEY HIM in overdrive.... and watch God move on our behalf... Attitude is everything!!! NotPerfectButWorthIt!!! Stay Blessed!!!

Remember kindness is the oil that takes the friction out of life. Heavenly Father, help me to put on Your garment of love so that I am prepared for whatever life brings me today. Attitude is everything!!! NotPerfectButWorthIt!!! Stay Blessed!!!

Remember take time to be "Thankful" for those that inspire, encourage, and make you a better you and in turn inspire, encourage, and make someone else be better for themselves! Attitude is everything!!! NotPerfectButWorthIt!!! Stay Blessed!!!

Remember be willing to obey God even if you don't feel up to it. He has great things in store for you! Just step out on a leap of faith, and allow God to do the rest. Attitude is everything!!! NotPerfectButWorthIt!!! Stay Blessed!!!

Remember if God has placed a "Vision" in your spirit and you come into agreement with him than NOTHING should stop you from activating it....
You do know that you're the only reason that the "Vision" has been activated, plain for others to view, but more importantly so that God receives the Glory! Attitude is everything!!! NotPerfectButWorthIt!!! Stay Blessed!!!

Remember try saying this today...." Something good is going to happen through me today... Attitude is everything!!! NotPerfectButWorthIt!!! Stay Blessed!!!

Remember I know we want and expect something good to happen to us, but how about allowing something good to happen through you to someone else.... Attitude is everything!!! NotPerfectButWorthIt!!! Stay Blessed!!!

Remember never feel pressured to do something that doesn't give you the peace of God as a Christian. It could be a good and honorable thing, but if you don't have peace about it wait for God to lead....; especially for married couples. Anything you do for God should have an ease to it, and never an anxious uneasy feeling.... Regret; try to avoid having it completely. We can't change the past, but we can learn from it, and continue to move forward! Attitude is everything!!! NotPerfectButWorthIt!!! Stay Blessed!!!

Remember let's be honest none of us like to change our environments because we become comfortable and content.... We hold on to people and/or situations beyond their purpose. When our environments no longer blesses us then we need an upgrade! An upgrade doesn't mean that the past was not necessary it just means it is no longer required. What will you consider upgrading? Attitude is everything!!! NotPerfectButWorthIt!!! Stay Blessed!!!

Remember just because you have acknowledged that God is your only source of strength and help; he will respond! Attitude is everything!!! NotPerfectButWorthIt!!! Stay Blessed!!!

Remember God's love for us is revealed through Jesus. Heavenly Father, thank You for loving me and pursuing a relationship with me. Help me to be a JOY to YOU by drawing near to YOU. Attitude is everything!!! NotPerfectButWorthIt!!! Stay Blessed!!!

Remember A LITTLE CAN MEAN SO MUCH! Next time you contemplate giving or doing something for someone just remember that just giving or doing a little can mean so much to those in need. Attitude is everything!!! NotPerfectButWorthIt!!! Stay Blessed!!!

Remember Do you know what makes God "Laugh..." when you take the time to "Plan" your life.... God down right chuckles....when you decide to plan out things for your life... instead of allowing him to guide and direct you... It's far better to make God smile and be happy when we trust him to be the "Guide" and we become the obedient "Followers....." Attitude is everything!!! NotPerfectButWorthIt!!! Stay Blessed!!!

Remember I was supposed to be a "Wreck"; I was supposed to be "Taken Out", but God said, "NOT SO....!" God stepped in and picked me up out of my mess/sin, and placed my feet on his solid ground; he turned me around, and now he is "Perfecting Me" into his own image. I am not perfect, but I am better today than I was yesterday or years before. God did this for me, and he will do the same for you, so TRY GOD; allow him to work in you what he has worked in me.... Attitude is everything!!! NotPerfectButWorthIt!!! Stay Blessed!!!

Remember I believe that God wants to save us all and bless us all, but when we accept him as our Savior then we are "Charged" with becoming "Change Agents" for him... So let's begin and/or continue to be "Change Agents" for the lost assisting them to become like us "Change Agents" for Christ! Attitude is everything!!! NotPerfectButWorthIt!!! Stay Blessed!!!

Remember When you've been hurt or offended, sometimes it's tempting to hold on to unforgiveness. But we have to remember, when people wrong us, our battle is not against flesh and blood. In other words, that person who hurt you is not the real enemy. The Bible says that your adversary is the devil, and he knows that if you don't forgive, your prayers won't be effective. Unforgiveness puts up a barrier in your life to the power of God. In fact, if we don't forgive others, we can't be forgiven by God. However, when you choose forgiveness, you open the door for God's healing power to flow through you! Attitude is everything!!! NotPerfectButWorthIt!!! Stay Blessed!!!

Remember When God's way becomes your way, you're on your way to great peace and joy. What's your way going to be? I am desiring my ways to be God's..... Attitude is everything!!! NotPerfectButWorthIt!!! Stay Blessed!!!

Remember to turn your doubts into shouts of joy, believe in yourself because no one can stop you but you!!! Attitude is everything!!! NotPerfectButWorthIt!!! Stay Blessed!!!

Remember being patient is not easy. We want quick and fast, but we need to take the time to build our foundation because quick and fast never last. A strong foundation is key in the process and what's a better foundation to build off than God!!! Attitude is everything!!! NotPerfectButWorthIt!!! Stay Blessed!!!

Remember waking up this morning is motivation enough. Now make it a great day and be a blessing to someone!!! Attitude is everything!!! NotPerfectButWorthIt!!! Stay Blessed!!!

Remember life is a gift so treat it as it is so. We are so spoiled and ungrateful sometimes like a child that doesn't understand. Be thankful and live it to the fullest!!! Attitude is everything!!! NotPerfectButWorthIt!!! Stay Blessed!!!

Remember to tell someone how good God has been to you today, and if they don't believe it say well I'm still here right!!! Attitude is everything!!! NotPerfectButWorthIt!!! Stay Blessed!!!

Remember to be excited not just because it's Friday, but because God is working in your favor!!! Attitude is everything!!! NotPerfectButWorthIt!!! Stay Blessed!!!

Remember to eliminate all distractions in your life. You have a mission to fulfill. Stay focused and keep it positive!!! Attitude is everything!!! NotPerfectButWorthIt!!! Stay Blessed!!!

Remember sometimes it take a beat down to bring out that leader in you!!! I pray this message encourage someone today because it sure encourages me!!! Attitude is everything!!! NotPerfectButWorthIt!!! Stay Blessed!!!

Remember let's always lift each other up!!! Attitude is everything!!! NotPerfectButWorthIt!!! Stay Blessed!!!

Remember your worst day with God will be better than your best day without Him, so stay connected!!! Attitude is everything!!! NotPerfectButWorthIt!!! Stay Blessed!!!

Remember God wants to be famous so tell someone everyday how good he has been to you so he gets his glory and watch how your day become that much better!!! Attitude is everything!!! NotPerfectButWorthIt!!! Stay Blessed!!!

Remember going through the process is the only way to get it done. There's no way around it, there's no shortcuts. Embrace it and trust it. Watch God bring you through stronger than ever!!! Attitude is everything!!! NotPerfectButWorthIt!!! Stay Blessed!!!

Remember nothing can stop God's plan for your life. The only hard thing we have to do is have patience. The rest is easy as long as we stay connected!!! Attitude is everything!!! NotPerfectButWorthIt!!! Stay Blessed!!!

Remember you may not feel blessed today but if you get in agreement with God and get a picture of yourself blessed you are going to move toward it. You need to see yourself blessed!!! Attitude is everything!!! NotPerfectButWorthIt!!! Stay Blessed!!!

Remember put to work the gift that God gave you. We all have different gifts but I'm speaking about the one we all have and that's your beautiful smile. It will be contagious and affective today!!! Attitude is everything!!! NotPerfectButWorthIt!!! Stay Blessed!!!

Remember anything in your way from being fruitful is a curse. The bible says you will have what you say. Just keep your faith!!! Attitude is everything!!! NotPerfectButWorthIt!!! Stay Blessed!!!

Remember we have developed the mindset to say thank God it's Friday!!! We should be thanking God for everyday because tomorrow is not promised. Being thankful is a positive attitude to have!!! Attitude is everything!!! NotPerfectButWorthIt!!! Stay Blessed!!!

Remember be careful who you allow in your life because negative people will subtract from your life. It's really that simple. Keep adding Positively!!! Attitude is everything!!! NotPerfectButWorthIt!!! Stay Blessed!!!

Remember stop waiting for the perfect time to start whatever you want to do because the perfect time is when you start. Have faith and move forward with it!!! Attitude is everything!!! NotPerfectButWorthIt!!! Stay Blessed!!!

Remember there's nothing in your way but you. It's just like lifting weights keep pushing until you can't push no more!!! Attitude is everything!!! NotPerfectButWorthIt!!! Stay Blessed!!!

Remember you will see the results in your life. You're unstoppable in all you do!!! Attitude is everything!!! NotPerfectButWorthIt!!! Stay Blessed!!!

Remember be excited for yourself as well as for someone else. Blessings are coming your way and I'm excited for you.

Just be ready to receive them!!! Attitude is everything!!! NotPerfectButWorthIt!!! Stay Blessed!!!

Remember we are not perfect but YES we are worth it!!! Let somebody know today that they are worth it because you don't know what they are going through but they are worth it no matter what anyone says!!! Attitude is everything!!! NotPerfectButWorthIt!!! Stay Blessed!!!

Remember that hard times come to pass not to stay so whatever you're going through you will make it through. Just continue to stand strong!!! Attitude is everything!!! NotPerfectButWorthIt!!! Stay Blessed!!!

Remember we complain so much we sometimes forget how blessed we are. Let's change our complaints to gratitude!!! Attitude is everything!!! NotPerfectButWorthIt!!! Stay Blessed!!!

Remember you don't have to stand in the rain, as days come and go so does the rain in your life. Chose to make your day a sunny one regardless of what's going on. Nothing gets accomplished by standing in the rain complaining. Trust that God is working it out for you!!! Attitude is everything!!! NotPerfectButWorthIt!!! Stay Blessed!!!

Remember we need to look at Monday's as 3 things, New Week, New Opportunities and More blessings coming our way. Attitude is everything!!! NotPerfectButWorthIt!!! Stay Blessed!!!

Remember we need to activate our faith every single day. As faith builds your confidence knowing you will make it through the day no matter what you face. Not allowing negatively in your space. Walk in it, Talk in it. Let your faith shine so bright it touches others!!! Attitude is everything!!! NotPerfectButWorthIt!!! Stay Blessed!!!

Remember always try to remember that God place people in your life for a season. As that season goes so does that person. Sometimes it's not easy to let go and you want to stay in that season, but seasons come and go. Let go and let God because in comes a better season!!! Attitude is everything!!! NotPerfectButWorthIt!!! Stay Blessed!!!

Remember with peace comes joy and there's nothing that can break that bond. So there's nothing that can break you when God is in the mist!!! Attitude is everything!!! NotPerfectButWorthIt!!! Stay Blessed!!!

Remember just continue to be encouraged as you start out your new week. There will be road blocks trying to get in your way, but you will get the victory over every single one. It's all about how you react to them!!! Attitude is everything!!! NotPerfectButWorthIt!!! Stay Blessed!!!

Remember thanking God for another day not just because it's Friday. Let's not take it for granted because it wasn't that alarm clock. God will continue to shine on you. God may change your direction but he never changes his promise!!!

Attitude is everything!!! NotPerfectButWorthIt!!! Stay Blessed!!!

Remember continue to stride in what you are chasing and let no one tell you it's too hard for you to achieve. If it was easy everyone would do what you do, but remember you have a calling on your life keep going!!! Attitude is everything!!! NotPerfectButWorthIt!!! Stay Blessed!!!

Remember just continue to be grateful because we have another day to get it right. We're not perfect but worth it. We watched God's amazing work this morning as the sun came up and realized how blessed we really are no matter our situation because it too shall pass!!! Keep your joy!!! Attitude is everything!!! NotPerfectButWorthIt!!! Stay Blessed!!!

Remember all you can do is continue to push forward and God will do the rest. Believe it and Claim it!!! Prayer changes things!!! Attitude is everything!!! NotPerfectButWorthIt!!! Stay Blessed!!!

Remember plant yourself in something positive, because negative weeds grow all around you, and will weigh you down if you allow it!!! Have a positive and productive day!!! Attitude is everything!!! NotPerfectButWorthIt!!! Stay Blessed!!!

Remember your life is a blessing. Stay grateful and continue to affect all you come in contact with in a positive way!!!

Attitude is everything!!! NotPerfectButWorthIt!!! Stay Blessed!!!

Remember don't get confused about who kept you!!! As we start this new week continue to be the best you. People will test you, things may go wrong but stay the best you and you will make it through!!! Attitude is everything!!! NotPerfectButWorthIt!!! Stay Blessed!!!

Remember faith can conquer fear. You only need to have a little faith to step out and be you. Just let your walk do your talk!!! Attitude is everything!!! NotPerfectButWorthIt!!! Stay Blessed!!!

Remember Everyday feed your mind and spirit with positive things and positive things will happen!!! Attitude is everything!!! NotPerfectButWorthIt!!! Stay Blessed!!!

Remember we know a God bigger than opinions, "say let people say what they want to say." Stay focused and make it an awesome day!!! Attitude is everything!!! NotPerfectButWorthIt!!! Stay Blessed!!!

Remember no matter how difficult a situation you may be facing today; God can turn it around. Just trust and believe!!! Attitude is everything!!! NotPerfectButWorthIt!!! Stay Blessed!!!

Remember look for an opportunity to make someone's day and put a smile on their face. You never know what kind of day they are having and your positive vibe can change everything for them. Then watch how it comes back if there's a day you need that!!! Attitude is everything!!! NotPerfectButWorthIt!!! Stay Blessed!!!

Remember the best thing is your possibilities are endless. Let's get this week started!!! Attitude is everything!!! NotPerfectButWorthIt!!! Stay Blessed!!!

Remember patience is a hard thing, but the reward at the end of it will be great. Don't judge your life around nobody else. Your blessing is coming!!! Attitude is everything!!! NotPerfectButWorthIt!!! Stay Blessed!!!

Remember be courageous in everything you do each day and watch the difference it makes in your life!!! Attitude is everything!!! NotPerfectButWorthIt!!! Stay Blessed!!!

Remember a positive mindset brings an amazing attitude. A can do attitude, a don't quit attitude. Just imagine if Jesus would have quit at the cross!!! So keep pushing through whatever you're going through it will past!!! Attitude is everything!!! NotPerfectButWorthIt!!! Stay Blessed!!!

Remember the world is designed to have its challenges, but there's no challenge that God can't get you through. Refusing to forfeit my joy and happiness!!! Attitude is everything!!! NotPerfectButWorthIt!!! Stay Blessed!!!

Remember step out with confidence you have a God that loves you, so you can do whatever it is you want to do. Just have patience!!! Attitude is everything!!! NotPerfectButWorthIt!!! Stay Blessed!!!

Remember that no one can take your joy and happiness but you. Attitude is everything!!! NotPerfectButWorthIt!!! Stay Blessed!!!

Remember be grateful for moments because they come and go, but last a lifetime in yours and someone you've touched mind!!! Attitude is everything!!! NotPerfectButWorthIt!!! Stay Blessed!!!

Remember as you know life is about choices and I truly believe if you choose to be happy you can be. Sometimes it seems we focus too much on the bad things rather than the good things. Live a grateful life and you will find joy!!! Attitude is everything!!! NotPerfectButWorthIt!!! Stay Blessed!!!

Remember if you decide to have a good day you will because no one can bring you down. Be bold with it and just smile!!! Attitude is everything!!! NotPerfectButWorthIt!!! Stay Blessed!!!

Remember Lord if I only encourage one person today I did what I needed to do. Just continue to stand on God's word whatever it is you are going through. He does have big plans for you!!! Attitude is everything!!! NotPerfectButWorthIt!!! Stay Blessed!!!

Remember God doesn't give us what we can handle, God helps us handle what we are given. So you are stronger than you think!!! Attitude is everything!!! NotPerfectButWorthIt!!! Stay Blessed!!!

Remember things happen in life that we can't control but we can control how we react to it!!! Attitude is everything!!! NotPerfectButWorthIt!!! Stay Blessed!!!

Remember no doubt it's by the Lord's grace we are still here. So make the best of it day by day!!! Attitude is everything!!! NotPerfectButWorthIt!!! Stay Blessed!!!

Remember you will never get a different result if you don't change something in your life. So change isn't always bad. See the positive things in change!!! Attitude is everything!!! NotPerfectButWorthIt!!! Stay Blessed!!!

Remember we're so quick to grab on to the negative that we can't see the positive. Change your mindset and be thankful so negatively can't win!!! Attitude is everything!!! NotPerfectButWorthIt!!! Stay Blessed!!!

Remember challenge yourself to be a better you going into this new week. Remember the small things we miss can make a big change!!! Attitude is everything!!! NotPerfectButWorthIt!!! Stay Blessed!!!

Remember we may have stressful days but we have a God to release that stress to. He's right there with us, so vent to him if you need to. Put your burdens in his hands and he knows exactly what to do with them with no judgement. People may not understand what you are going through but God does and he got you. Stand on it and believe that!!! Attitude is everything!!! NotPerfectButWorthIt!!! Stay Blessed!!!

Remember patience is one of the hardest things to have. We want things to happen for us right away, but I believe there's a lesson inside of patience and that's to trust in the Lord. Yes, it's easier said than done but keep that FAITH!!! Attitude is everything!!! NotPerfectButWorthIt!!! Stay Blessed!!!

Remember why should we give up on ourselves? God refuses to give up on us. Yes, we make mistakes but thank God for his mercy and grace. You are more than a conqueror. Recognize the power you have inside of you. Who can stop you with God on your side. Refuse to let anyone bring you down. In the name of Jesus declare your victory today!!! Attitude is everything!!! NotPerfectButWorthIt!!! Stay Blessed!!!

Remember that hanging with positive people gets positive results, not all so called friends are good for you. Using good judgment will hurt the flesh sometimes but save your soul. Don't compromise and accept a poor substitute for the greatness that God has coming for you!!! Attitude is everything!!! NotPerfectButWorthIt!!! Stay Blessed!!!

Remember never get tired of praying because prayer does change things. Lord I'm praying right now in the name of Jesus to be a hedge of protection around everyone. Keep them safe and covered as they go out and start their new week. Amen. Take a minute to pray for someone today we all need it!!! Attitude is everything!!! NotPerfectButWorthIt!!! Stay Blessed!!!

Remember don't lose hope. Yes, it's hard and yes it's crazy out here. Losing hope is what the enemy want you to do and then he wins because now you're hopeless. Things can't change unless you walk your talk. Complaining and stressing over things changes nothing. Stop waiting for something to happen and then talk about it. Yes I said talk about it; there's more talk than action. Who's going to stand up? We have become a world that's so full of selfish people it's ridiculous; until it hits home nobody cares. It's amazing. When we decide to come together and touch and agree, we are more powerful than you know. Regardless of what's going on God is still God!!! Attitude is everything!!! NotPerfectButWorthIt!!! Stay Blessed!!!

Remember don't be so focused on what you want that you take for granted what you have. You have been blessed with what you need. So be thankful!!! Attitude is everything!!! NotPerfectButWorthIt!!! Stay Blessed!!!

Remember no need to over think things, pray about it and leave it in God hands. He knows exactly what to do. He will carry your burdens and let you be stress free. Now that you prayed about it go and have an awesome day!!! Attitude is everything!!! NotPerfectButWorthIt!!! Stay Blessed!!!

Remember don't be controlled by any circumstance because they come and go, tough times don't last tough people do. Stand and believe that!!! Attitude is everything!!! NotPerfectButWorthIt!!! Stay Blessed!!!

Remember just in case you are feeling weak this morning and feel like you don't have the strength to make it through the day keep this in mind. I can't speak for everybody but I need God every day to make it through the day!!! Attitude is everything!!! NotPerfectButWorthIt!!! Stay Blessed!!!

Remember to challenge yourself today to let nothing get in your way or nothing upset you. Set your mind right now say to yourself, you are somebody; you are loved; you have the potential to affect eternity, God loves you and I believe he has something special for you. Stand on it and believe that!!! Attitude is everything!!! NotPerfectButWorthIt!!! Stay Blessed!!!

Remember it's a new day and your boss is on your back already and things are not going your way and it's not even 12:00 o'clock. You may have a reason to sit around and pout but you don't have a right to because Jesus paid a heavy price for us to stand up strong and be great. Be grateful you're here and make the best of it!!! Attitude is everything!!! NotPerfectButWorthIt!!! Stay Blessed!!!

Remember it might not make much sense now whatever it is your going through but God is behind the scene putting in that work just for you. One thing I know is you will come out better and stronger!!! Attitude is everything!!! NotPerfectButWorthIt!!! Stay Blessed!!!

Remember don't forget take time to enjoy life, time goes so fast and we miss so much. Notice how we say all the time can Friday please get here not realizing that we are rushing through our lives and we can never get that time back. What a stressful way to live. Slow down and go through the process that God has you in. Stay positive and keep the negativity far away from you!!! Attitude is everything!!! NotPerfectButWorthIt!!! Stay Blessed!!!

Remember to resist the enemy and he will flee. He will try you to see what kind a mood you're in. Stay positive and try not to get caught up in what hasn't happened yet for you and think of all the things that have happened for you. God is working. Stand and believe that!!! Attitude is everything!!! NotPerfectButWorthIt!!! Stay Blessed!!!

Remember great things happens when you allow God to work through you and lead you. Better decisions with a different mindset. Seek him for answers and you will find them. In him is where you find your peace not in man. We can't please everyone so stop trying, focus more on pleasing God!!! Attitude is everything!!! NotPerfectButWorthIt!!! Stay Blessed!!!

Remember don't miss your blessing. We spend way too much time complaining about this and that and never see our blessing. I've learn in life and still learning that complaining changes nothing but PRAYER changes everything. We just need to be patient. Don't allow your feelings to control your destiny!!! Attitude is everything!!! NotPerfectButWorthIt!!! Stay Blessed!!!

Remember your actions will always follow your beliefs. So it's your choice to what you choose to believe in your life. One of God's greatest gifts to us is free will!!! Attitude is everything!!! NotPerfectButWorthIt!!! Stay Blessed!!!

Remember to try and focus on the good things and not the bad things. The possibilities and not the problems, just imagine if God only focus on our bad things. "Whoa" Thank God for Grace and Mercy. If it wasn't for that where would we be? So bad things and problems will come but rest in him. Stand and believe that!!! Attitude is everything!!! NotPerfectButWorthIt!!! Stay Blessed!!!

Remember make sure you take time out to be thankful to the one who made us. We belong to God not the world and we are absolutely nothing without him. Lord cover us as we deal with the negative things of this world, the enemy will try us but let us not fall. Let's start this week out right and on a positive note!!! Attitude is everything!!! NotPerfectButWorthIt!!! Stay Blessed!!!

Remember you already know that life is about choices, so you can choose to sit around and complain about life is not fair or you can live in Faith and RISE up on any situation you facing. Your choice!!! Attitude is everything!!! NotPerfectButWorthIt!!! Stay Blessed!!!

Remember stop wasting your time thinking about things you can't control. What good does it do walking around being miserable and having a funky attitude that no one wants to be around. Keep the good things on your mind because you can control that and how you carry yourself. Positive thoughts Positive results!!! Attitude is everything!!! NotPerfectButWorthIt!!! Stay Blessed!!!

Remember nothing compares to God, get it in your head devil you can't win. Push us down and we get back up because we stand on the word. We refuse to let you win so in the name of Jesus flee. Allow nothing to steal your joy. Today is going to be a great day. Stand and believe that!!! Attitude is everything!!! NotPerfectButWorthIt!!! Stay Blessed!!!

Remember to keep the right attitude and walk in Faith NOT Fear. The enemy will put the pressure on you to do something you shouldn't do or say something you shouldn't say. We already know that so we should already be prepared not to act out of our character. Continue to strive to be a better person each of you will have victory and peace. Faith comes by hearing, and hearing by the word of God!!! Attitude is everything!!! NotPerfectButWorthIt!!! Stay Blessed!!!

Remember never confuse the mission between man and God. What God has planned for you is way better than your plan. So endure the process you're going through. You might be going through a lot but God is just making your testimony more powerful than you can ever imagine. You might feel alone but he is with you. Step forward with him as your foundation because there's no other rock stronger. Belief begins the blessing. Thank you Jesus!!! Attitude is everything!!! NotPerfectButWorthIt!!! Stay Blessed!!!

Remember to stretch yourself today because with God there is no limit. Plant yourself on good ground and watch how you grow. The gift inside of you is meant for the world to see. Nothing can stop what God has touched, so be fearless and put your faith out front!!! Attitude is everything!!! NotPerfectButWorthIt!!! Stay Blessed!!!

Remember If God is for us who can be against us. No sickness, No debt, No haters, No bad bosses, No negative people. Absolutely nothing. Nothing intimidates God!!! Attitude is everything!!! NotPerfectButWorthIt!!! Stay Blessed!!!

Remember to wake up with more praise and less worry and watch how your day goes!!! Attitude is everything!!! NotPerfectButWorthIt!!! Stay Blessed!!!

Remember nothing to fear, have faith because when God has his hand on you he got you covered!!! Attitude is everything!!! NotPerfectButWorthIt!!! Stay Blessed!!!

Remember it's not just another morning, it's another morning we are blessed to get it right. So don't waste this day with a bad attitude and a stone face. Instead smile, be grateful and the bright spot in the place!!! Attitude is everything!!! NotPerfectButWorthIt!!! Stay Blessed!!!

Remember know your worth and don't settle, Jesus thought we were worth dying for. So why concern yourself what people think your worth is when he already showed us our worth!!! Attitude is everything!!! NotPerfectButWorthIt!!! Stay Blessed!!!

Remember don't stay in the place of your hurt and disappointment trying to fix it or resolve it, shake it off!!! God always has a new season, a new assignment, and a new opportunity for us, so stand on and believe that truth if we truly want to shake off the dust!!! Attitude is everything!!! NotPerfectButWorthIt!!! Stay Blessed!!!

Remember to take on every new day with an attitude of winning, and no one can stop you or bring you down. Watch what kind of day you have then!!! Attitude is everything!!! NotPerfectButWorthIt!!! Stay Blessed!!!

Remember the change starts with you. Talking about it won't change it, only action. Your attitude can take you up or bring you down. So put your attitude in check and keep it positive!!! Attitude is everything!!! NotPerfectButWorthIt!!! Stay Blessed!!!

Remember you can find something good when things go wrong. Unfortunately, bad things happen, but we have to be strong enough to overcome those things, and it starts with our attitude and the way we handle things!!! Attitude is everything!!! NotPerfectButWorthIt!!! Stay Blessed!!!

Remember if you stop pushing now you will never actually know how many steps are really left to your destiny. So keep going!!! Attitude is everything!!! NotPerfectButWorthIt!!! Stay Blessed!!!

Remember that you can't succeed if you never try. So never lose sight of the prize. What you are going through is just part of your process to success!!! NotPerfectButWorthIt

Remember don't allow anyone to tell you that you are reaching too high or you are dreaming too big, there is no limitation when your foundation is built off of God!!! Attitude is everything!!! NotPerfectButWorthIt!!! Stay Blessed!!!

Remember don't be fooled into thinking you can do anything without God. The enemy wants you to think that so he shows you only what he wants you to see. Try and look past that moment of satisfying your flesh in any way. We cannot do this in our own strength, it's ok to lean on God!!! Attitude is everything!!! NotPerfectButWorthIt!!! Stay Blessed!!!

Remember knowing something and doing something are two different things. You know that God blessed you with a unique gift so now it's time to do something with that

gift!!! Attitude is everything!!! NotPerfectButWorthIt!!!
Stay Blessed!!!

Remember just in case you are wondering why you choose
to help someone else in need when you are going through
your own need; is simply because you are trusting God is
working it out for your good. That's living a Faith Life so keep
living!!! Attitude is everything!!! NotPerfectButWorthIt!!!
Stay Blessed!!!

Remember when life's pressure gets too heavy, Jesus is the
best spotter to have when it comes to lifting a lot of weight
off of you!!! Attitude is everything!!! NotPerfectButWorthIt!!!
Stay Blessed!!!

Remember even if we fall we still can move forward because
we knew how to crawl before we could walk. We all fall
sometimes so getting back up shouldn't be a problem!!!
Attitude is everything!!! NotPerfectButWorthIt!!! Stay
Blessed!!!

Remember you're STILL STANDING even after the enemy
tried to sit you down. Nothing like mercy and grace. God is
that good!!! Attitude is everything!!! NotPerfectButWorthIt!!!
Stay Blessed!!!

Remember to trust the process and don't give up. Don't allow
anyone to say you can't when you can. God placed something
special in each and every one of us that no one can take it

anyway. Stand firm he got us!!! Attitude is everything!!! NotPerfectButWorthIt!!! Stay Blessed!!!

Remember to be used today. Not by people but by God so that he can reach people. Smile and tell someone it's going to be a great day for you, big things are coming your way just continue to stand on his promise. Now understand that's for each and every one of us!!! Attitude is everything!!! NotPerfectButWorthIt!!! Stay Blessed!!!

Remember to start your morning out with God by thanking him for another day. A grateful heart is hard to break as long as you keep in mind what's at stake. The enemy is after your soul!!! Attitude is everything!!! NotPerfectButWorthIt!!! Stay Blessed!!!

Remember running to man is a quick fix for the moment but running to God is peace and joy at full term!!! Attitude is everything!!! NotPerfectButWorthIt!!! Stay Blessed!!!

Remember stay in your lane and let God work. His plan is better than our plan. He made it even before we were born!!! Attitude is everything!!! NotPerfectButWorthIt!!! Stay Blessed!!!

Remember to watch your blind side. That's your weakness where the enemy likes to attack. Where we are weak God is strong!!! Attitude is everything!!! NotPerfectButWorthIt!!! Stay Blessed!!!

Remember apart from God we can do nothing but with him we can do anything. Stand strong and keep your faith and everything will be alright!!! Attitude is everything!!! NotPerfectButWorthIt!!! Stay Blessed!!!

Remember If we treated everyday like Friday just imagine what kind of attitude we would have every day and if we had the attitude of Christ just imagine how the world can change!!! Attitude is everything!!! NotPerfectButWorthIt!!! Stay Blessed!!!

Remember in your climb towards Christ and your purpose you are going to lose people but you've come too far to give up now. Keep climbing even if you lose everyone you will never be alone!!! Attitude is everything!!! NotPerfectButWorthIt!!! Stay Blessed!!!

Remember the extra mile isn't as far as you think. So keep moving you're almost exactly where God wants you. His will!!! Attitude is everything!!! NotPerfectButWorthIt!!! Stay Blessed!!!

Remember things happen and life goes on regardless of how we feel. We can't let our emotions control our attitude. A lot of things change but the word of God remains the same. When doubt creeps in go to that word and stand on his promise.!!! Attitude is everything!!! NotPerfectButWorthIt!!! Stay Blessed!!!

Remember never compromise your joy, it's hard to upset someone that's at peace and you can find your peace in him. For he is the prince of peace. Stay connected!!! Attitude is everything!!! NotPerfectButWorthIt!!! Stay Blessed!!!

Remember there's no limit to what God can do, so don't try to put him in a box. Allow him to have room to work in your life. Keep your faith in the right place!!! Attitude is everything!!! NotPerfectButWorthIt!!! Stay Blessed!!!

Remember God didn't give up on you, so don't you ever give up on you, he has big plans for you so stay rooted in his love. Where would we be if not for his grace!!! Attitude is everything!!! NotPerfectButWorthIt!!! Stay Blessed!!!

Remember God doesn't take us through things to make you weak. It's to make us strong. So we're already battle tested when the test comes and strapped with the greatest weapon in him!!! Attitude is everything!!! NotPerfectButWorthIt!!! Stay Blessed!!!

Remember God is a God of newness, so why worry about your past. Continue to push forward into the greatness he has for you!!! Attitude is everything!!! NotPerfectButWorthIt!!! Stay Blessed!!!

Remember no one is off limits, the enemy attacks every single one of us. Here is the good news God has already warned us so we shouldn't be surprised. God has already prepared us. We need to just trust in his word and keep our

Faith!!! Attitude is everything!!! NotPerfectButWorthIt!!! Stay Blessed!!!

Remember God can give you the grace to go through things, so instead of giving up allow it to make you strong and push through!!! Attitude is everything!!! NotPerfectButWorthIt!!! Stay Blessed!!!

Remember stop looking for a savior in man, you have already been saved!!! Attitude is everything!!! NotPerfectButWorthIt!!! Stay Blessed!!!

Remember we might be imperfect people but we know and serve a perfect God. Thank God for his mercy and grace every day you wake up and watch the difference in your attitude switch!!! Attitude is everything!!! NotPerfectButWorthIt!!! Stay Blessed!!!

Remember when those you love see your dependence on God, it will help them depend on him as well. So when you're going through a storm call on him not man. Attitude is everything!!! NotPerfectButWorthIt!!! Stay Blessed!!!

Remember we don't have to wait until Sunday to praise his name, take time every day to praise the name above all names. Didn't he keep you? Didn't he wake you up this morning? There's absolutely nothing that he can't do. Stay grateful. Attitude is everything!!! NotPerfectButWorthIt!!! Stay Blessed!!!

Remember don't hide your struggles from the one who can keep you struggle free. Keep your faith and stand completely on his word!!! Attitude is everything!!! NotPerfectButWorthIt!!! Stay Blessed!!!

Remember we were born with greatness because we are created in his image. So don't get loss in so much negativity that you can't find something positive going on. He is a God of peace!!! Attitude is everything!!! NotPerfectButWorthIt!!! Stay Blessed!!!

Remember worrying is the result of wrong thinking. Worrying + Complaining = Stress

Trusting + Faith = Peace

Now you decide your math!!! Attitude is everything!!! NotPerfectButWorthIt!!! Stay Blessed!!!

Remember if you put your trust in God you can be at peace, no matter what you're going through!!! Attitude is everything!!! NotPerfectButWorthIt!!! Stay Blessed!!!

Remember the sacrifice he made for us. He paid a debit we couldn't afford to pay. So stay humble and grateful!!! Thank you Jesus!!! Attitude is everything!!! NotPerfectButWorthIt!!! Stay Blessed!!!

Remember as we leave out the year and go into a new year. God stays with us, so we are already winning. Now that doesn't mean that we won't have our challenges, it only means our challenges won't be and can't be bigger than our GOD!!! Attitude is everything!!! NotPerfectButWorthIt!!! Stay Blessed!!!

Remember it's hard to understand something you haven't been through, so show people the love of Christ, it makes a difference in their day. Attitude is everything!!! NotPerfectButWorthIt!!! Stay Blessed!!!

Remember to stand strong and shine bright each and every day because God loves us!!! Attitude is everything!!! NotPerfectButWorthIt!!! Stay Blessed!!!

Remember it doesn't have to be Thanksgiving to be thankful, we have 364 more days to be thankful for!!! Attitude is everything!!! NotPerfectButWorthIt!!! Stay Blessed!!!

Remember the first decision you should make every day when you wake up is to talk to God. Prayer changes things and can set the tone of your day. New week, new tone!!! God is amazing!!! Attitude is everything!!! NotPerfectButWorthIt!!! Stay Blessed!!!

Remember even through the pain you can make it. You just have to BELIEVE!!! God is always in control and on the throne. Stand on and believe that. Attitude is everything!!! Attitude is everything!!! NotPerfectButWorthIt!!! Stay Blessed!!!

Remember it only takes a few minutes to pray that can change your day. There's power in prayer. God loves our attention so show him some love each and every day. Attitude is everything!!! NotPerfectButWorthIt!!! Stay Blessed!!!

Remember to stay prayed up and connected to the source. When Peter took his eyes off of Jesus he started to sink into the ocean. A lot of us are sinking because we take our eyes off Jesus as soon as a little turbulence comes into our life. Stand strong and believe. Attitude is everything!!! NotPerfectButWorthIt!!! Stay Blessed!!!

Remember the grind of everyday life can sometimes be draining and can sometimes bring you down, but the good news is we have a God that can re-energize and lift us up!!! Attitude is everything!!! NotPerfectButWorthIt!!! Stay Blessed!!!

Remember if we base our worth on our abilities or approval of others, then our behavior will reflect the insecurity, fear, and anger that comes from such instability. Trust your worth in him and not people!!! Attitude is everything!!! NotPerfectButWorthIt!!! Stay Blessed!!!

Remember to stay focused. The enemy wants to distract you from your goals and doing God's will. Do not allow him to hinder your prayers. Continue to stand on firm on your Faith!!! Attitude is everything!!! NotPerfectButWorthIt!!! Stay Blessed!!!

Remember regardless of what day it is always praise his name. He is worthy of all our praise. Stay focused and be a blessing to someone. Attitude is everything!!! NotPerfectButWorthIt!!! Stay Blessed!!!

Remember even though we don't deserve it, God STILL loves us unconditionally and his plans for our lives are perfect. Allow God to do a work in you and through you!!! Attitude is everything!!! NotPerfectButWorthIt!!! Stay Blessed!!!

Remember learn to trust the process even if you don't understand it. God works in mysterious ways that has your mind racing a thousand miles an hour, but once you made it through it will be worth the process. Stand on and believe that!!! Attitude is everything!!! NotPerfectButWorthIt!!! Stay Blessed!!!

Remember to plant your feet into the ground and continue to move forward. Don't allow anyone to knock you out of your lane. Your life is what you choose to accept!!! Attitude is everything!!! NotPerfectButWorthIt!!! Stay Blessed!!!

Remember it's a new week, new tweak and whatever is in your way can't stay in the name of Jesus!!! Attitude is everything!!! NotPerfectButWorthIt!!! Stay Blessed!!!

Remember worry see's the problem but faith see's the solution. In other words, faith see's, the God that can handle the problem so there's no need to worry as long as you have faith. Stand on and believe that!!! Attitude is everything!!! NotPerfectButWorthIt!!! Stay Blessed!!!

Remember to spend time with God in the morning. Even if it's for a couple of minutes in prayer. He loves spending time with us. Trust me it will prepare you for your day ahead as long as you stay focused!!! Attitude is everything!!! NotPerfectButWorthIt!!! Stay Blessed!!!

Remember a promise from God means it's yours. Stand on and believe that!!! Attitude is everything!!! NotPerfectButWorthIt!!! Stay Blessed!!!

Remember don't be discouraged if things don't look like it's going your way. God gave you the gift and the vision, so keep building and pushing forward everything will work out as long as he is your foundation!!! Attitude is everything!!! NotPerfectButWorthIt!!! Stay Blessed!!!

Remember to step into a new week with a head full of steam and make yourself unstoppable. There will be roadblocks ahead but stay connected to the source to stay on course!!! Attitude is everything!!! NotPerfectButWorthIt!!! Stay Blessed!!!

Remember people come and go out your life and things always change, but one thing remains the same the word of God. He will never leave or forsake you. Stand and believe that!!! Attitude is everything!!! NotPerfectButWorthIt!!! Stay Blessed!!!

Remember in God's presence is where you will find your joy. So if you're having a bad day find yourself in his presence!!!

Attitude is everything!!! NotPerfectButWorthIt!!! Stay Blessed!!!

Remember God got you, so why allow anyone to tell you anything different. You are still here for a reason. Each and every one of us has a purpose. So when negative people try to weight you down just tell them I'm too busy being lifted up because God's got me!!! Attitude is everything!!! NotPerfectButWorthIt!!! Stay Blessed!!!

Remember not to go down the road with negative people. We already know that misery loves company. Instead bring them down your road of positivity. Because positive thoughts get better results. Stand on and believe that!!! Attitude is everything!!! NotPerfectButWorthIt!!! Stay Blessed!!!

Remember we must keep our emotions in control. The strength isn't in checking a person that did you wrong, the strength is in being able to resist!!! Attitude is everything!!! NotPerfectButWorthIt!!! Stay Blessed!!!

Remember your foundation is so important. You might can't see it but it holds everything up. Trust God as your foundation because there's no foundation stronger. Even though you can't see him he is always working behind the scenes to hold you up. So when you're going through something stand firm on your foundation!!! Attitude is everything!!! NotPerfectButWorthIt!!! Stay Blessed!!!

Remember to make good use of your time. Don't waste it watching and wondering what other people are doing, do you. God has different plans for everyone so get a hold onto your plan and run with it!!! Attitude is everything!!! NotPerfectButWorthIt!!! Stay Blessed!!!

Remember to give your best love while people are at their worst. Pray for people and watch how it changes things and situations!!! Attitude is everything!!! NotPerfectButWorthIt!!! Stay Blessed!!!

Remember we don't have to pretend that things don't get bad for us or we don't make mistakes because we're not perfect, but we know a perfect God and he got us covered. Tell all your haters and negative people that tries to surround you that God got you!!! Attitude is everything!!! NotPerfectButWorthIt!!! Stay Blessed!!!

Remember never miss an opportunity to thank God, he is the reason why you are breathing. It will change your whole attitude!!! Attitude is everything!!! NotPerfectButWorthIt!!! Stay Blessed!!!

Remember the lights don't really come on at your job until you get there, because you carry a light inside you that shines so bright that no one can put out. Let them see your Godly shine and watch how it reflects off all who's around you!!! Attitude is everything!!! NotPerfectButWorthIt!!! Stay Blessed!!!

Remember if problems come along continue to stand strong and keep your hands lifted. Stop telling God how big your problems are, instead tell your problems how big your God is!!! Attitude is everything!!! NotPerfectButWorthIt!!! Stay Blessed!!!

Remember to take time for yourself to see how beautiful God work is. It will put your mind at peace and there's nothing like peace from God!!! Attitude is everything!!! NotPerfectButWorthIt!!! Stay Blessed!!!

Remember never waste your time or a day to negativity. Stand strong and allow no one get you out of character. Know who the real enemy is and never let him take your joy!!! Attitude is everything!!! NotPerfectButWorthIt!!! Stay Blessed!!!

Remember in the Bible it says joy comes in the morning, so why trip about another morning. Try and understand it's a blessing to wake up. So your joy comes every morning you wake up no matter what day it is!!! Attitude is everything!!! NotPerfectButWorthIt!!! Stay Blessed!!!

Remember the more you start your day out with God and keep your focus on him. The more positives and love will flow out of you. With that, things in your life will have better results!!! Attitude is everything!!! NotPerfectButWorthIt!!! Stay Blessed!!!

Remember you don't have to react to every little thing. Show the enemy that you are rooted in God's love and negativity doesn't live inside you!!! Attitude is everything!!! NotPerfectButWorthIt!!! Stay Blessed!!!

Remember apart from God we can do nothing but with him we can do anything. Stand strong and keep your faith and everything will be alright!!! Attitude is everything!!! NotPerfectButWorthIt!!! Stay Blessed!!!

Remember stop worrying about being accepted and become an expert in ignoring negative people and thoughts. The Bible tells us to guard our minds, if the enemy can control our thinking he can control our life. Keep control of your life!!! Attitude is everything!!! NotPerfectButWorthIt!!! Stay Blessed!!!

Remember God's goal is not to force us to love him. He wants us to love him by choice. Just like he chooses to love us through it all. Our good and our bad. What's greater than the love of our creator!!! Attitude is everything!!! NotPerfectButWorthIt!!! Stay Blessed!!!

Remember you only get one opportunity for first impression, so why not impress someone with the love of Christ. That covers it all!!! Attitude is everything!!! NotPerfectButWorthIt!!! Stay Blessed!!!

Remember to embrace this new week with a grateful attitude. Carry that attitude so strong that when someone comes and tries to steal your joy the only thing they steal is that grateful attitude. So let the stealing begin!!! Attitude is everything!!! NotPerfectButWorthIt!!! Stay Blessed!!!

Remember there's nothing you're going through today that Jesus doesn't understand, he's here for us and loves us more than you know. Take time to understand what he went through just for you!!! Attitude is everything!!! NotPerfectButWorthIt!!! Stay Blessed!!!

Remember it's ok to ask the Lord to help guide you through your day because you will be tested. Big or small just allow him to work through you in any situation and he'll see you through it. Stand on and believe that!!! Attitude is everything!!! NotPerfectButWorthIt!!! Stay Blessed!!!

Remember you know your past, but God wants you to know a great future. Change is possible, and your future can be full of the life you always have desired. Start your change today and push toward your goals!!! Attitude is everything!!! NotPerfectButWorthIt!!! Stay Blessed!!!

Remember that through it all God will never leave you nor forsake you, and that's the solid foundation we need and can stand on for our life. Understand God loves us and desires a relationship with us. It's ok to fall in love again!!! Attitude is everything!!! NotPerfectButWorthIt!!! Stay Blessed!!!

Remember to be content, sometimes we wonder why other people get things that we would like to have and we don't, but forget that God is a gift to us and he's giving us far more than we deserve. So let's us keep in mind we have the greatest gift of all when we fill like complaining about things!!! Attitude is everything!!! NotPerfectButWorthIt!!! Stay Blessed!!!

Remember this is the day the Lord has made we will be glad and rejoice in it. Doesn't mean it has to be Sunday. We need to be glad and rejoice in every day because it's a blessing to wake up!!! Attitude is everything!!! NotPerfectButWorthIt!!! Stay Blessed!!!

Remember that the enemy sets you up to get upset. We have to look past that moment and see the better. Lean not on our understanding but trust in the Lord with all your heart!!! Attitude is everything!!! NotPerfectButWorthIt!!! Stay Blessed!!!

Encouragement

Remember When you're in new territory, use your GPS (God's Prayer Signals). Attitude is everything!!! NotPerfectButWorthIt!!! Stay Blessed!!!

Remember Are some "Hating" on you because of your color...? Yes, I said "color"; what I am referring to is the "BRIGHT COLOR OF GOD...." God's color is vibrant and shines very bright; so continue to be the COLOR of LIGHT, and SHINE BRIGHT in a dark dark world... Attitude is everything!!! NotPerfectButWorthIt!!! Stay Blessed!!!

Remember you are not responsible for what is to come in your future; you are only responsible for being faithful in doing God's work right now... Our reward is not based upon how much activity we have done, but how we have been faithful to what God has set before us. Attitude is everything!!! NotPerfectButWorthIt!!! Stay Blessed!!!

Remember never be shy about asking and continuing to ask God to meet all of your needs.

Father in heaven, thank You for the promise of Your help when we are tempted and for the truth that Satan's power is limited.

Give us the wisdom to recognize temptation and the humility to rely on Your Spirit for the strength to resist. AMEN! Attitude is everything!!! NotPerfectButWorthIt!!! Stay Blessed!!!

Remember a new day is God's way of saying One More Time, Go Make a Difference, touch a heart, encourage a Mind, Inspire a Soul and Enjoy the Day!!! Good Day and Be Blessed! Attitude is everything!!! NotPerfectButWorthIt!!! Stay Blessed!!!

Remember your worst day with God will be better than your best day without Him. The Holy Spirit is here to speak to you and help you in every way you need help.... Attitude is everything!!! NotPerfectButWorthIt!!! Stay Blessed!!!

Remember God loves you just the way you are and He will help you become what He wants you to be. Attitude is everything!!! NotPerfectButWorthIt!!! Stay Blessed!!!

Remember when we put our faith in "man"; they will "fail" you most every time... However, when you put your FAITH in God; he never fails.... his "Will" is perfect!!! Attitude is everything!!! NotPerfectButWorthIt!!! Stay Blessed!!!

Remember...God will do great things in your life as you continue to move forward with Him. Attitude is everything!!! NotPerfectButWorthIt!!! Stay Blessed!!!

Remember...Hallelujah...! It's the Highest Praise in honoring our God. Did you know that we often shout and cheer louder at sporting events, concerts, etc... on things that only satisfy us for the moment?!? Now, this may be a weird thought or concept, but what if...seriously just what if we all decided in the morning and throughout the day to shout out with a loud voice HALLELUJAH JESUS..... You would make God smile.... and the world would know how great our God is! Attitude is everything!!! NotPerfectButWorthIt!!! Stay Blessed!!!

Remember I hope it is your desire to aspire, inspire, and encourage with your words and actions on such a large platform as LIFE. Attitude is everything!!! NotPerfectButWorthIt!!! Stay Blessed!!!

Remember we often learn as children and adults to stop, drop, and roll when there is fire.... why not do the same when you experience a spiritual fire..., so when there is a fire in your life; stop, drop, and PRAY..... Jesus only dwells in peace! Attitude is everything!!! NotPerfectButWorthIt!!! Stay Blessed!!!

Remember God is the answer to your peace in the midst of life, etc.! Fight for your peace of mind through him! Attitude is everything!!! NotPerfectButWorthIt!!! Stay Blessed!!!

Remember Stop and drop to your knees and ask God to enter into the "Environment!" Attitude is everything!!! NotPerfectButWorthIt!!! Stay Blessed!!!

Remember God is not lost, so stop stating that I was looking for him. God is still and will always be present! Truth be told he found you! Attitude is everything!!! NotPerfectButWorthIt!!! Stay Blessed!!!

Remember God is not limited to the categories that the world attempts to use as identification. Attitude is everything!!! NotPerfectButWorthIt!!! Stay Blessed!!!

Remember our sin is great—God's grace is greater! Attitude is everything!!! NotPerfectButWorthIt!!! Stay Blessed!!!

Remember no matter if God chooses an "Easy Breakthrough deliverance" or a "Go Through deliverance" in your situation; it's all for your good, and the Glory and Honor is due to him. Attitude is everything!!! NotPerfectButWorthIt!!! Stay Blessed!!!

Remember praises going up to God means he begins to re-arranage your situation...for your good and his glory... Attitude is everything!!! NotPerfectButWorthIt!!! Stay Blessed!!!

Remember God sees all the good works you have done in secret and He will reward you. Attitude is everything!!! NotPerfectButWorthIt!!! Stay Blessed!!!

Remember Our knowledge will always be limited, but knowing God is what matters most. Attitude is everything!!! NotPerfectButWorthIt!!! Stay Blessed!!!

Remember God uses suffering to strengthen our faith. Thank You for assuring us that suffering is never wasted when we place our confidence in who You are, what You've done, and what You're capable of doing. Attitude is everything!!! NotPerfectButWorthIt!!! Stay Blessed!!!

Remember On today, I am here because of God, my family, and friends that surrounds me.... Attitude is everything!!! NotPerfectButWorthIt!!! Stay Blessed!!!

Remember What I am called to do is more important than where I came from... Attitude is everything!!! NotPerfectButWorthIt!!! Stay Blessed!!!

Remember Sometimes it is better to be a STRONG, CONFIDENT, and BOLD SECOND to something or someone then aiming to be the FIRST in everything... Attitude is everything!!! NotPerfectButWorthIt!!! Stay Blessed!!!

Remember People and things come into your life for either Blessings or Lessons! Attitude is everything!!! NotPerfectButWorthIt!!! Stay Blessed!!!

Remember God's people don't live in the spirit of FEAR, but in FAITH! Attitude is everything!!! NotPerfectButWorthIt!!! Stay Blessed!!!

Remember Contentment Brings Celebration! Comparison Kills Contentment! Attitude is everything!!! NotPerfectBut WorthIt!!! Stay Blessed!!!

Remember There's more to life than what happens to us; if you believe in he who can RESTORE! Attitude is everything!!! NotPerfectButWorthIt!!! Stay Blessed!!!

Remember Seasons are necessary....Spring, Summer, Fall, and Winter are required in our physical lives as it is in our spiritual lives... Some people and/or situations are that seasons......once they have fulfilled their purpose then the next season will occur.... Attitude is everything!!! NotPerfectButWorthIt!!! Stay Blessed!!!

Remember When you are critical of someone who is critical of you; you have allowed their sinful ways to enter you... Attitude is everything!!! NotPerfectButWorthIt!!! Stay Blessed!!!

Remember If you do the seeking, God will do the speaking. So get to seeking and investing into your personal relationship with him; he'll provide the answers just be open to receive them even if they are not what you expected to hear.... Attitude is everything!!! NotPerfectButWorthIt!!! Stay Blessed!!!

Remember God love for us is forever! Attitude is everything!!! NotPerfectButWorthIt!!! Stay Blessed!!!

Remember I am stronger than my flesh and my FAITH remains in control! AMEN! Attitude is everything!!! NotPerfectButWorthIt!!! Stay Blessed!!!

Remember It's not what other people call you that matters; it's only what God calls you and you respond to... Attitude is everything!!! NotPerfectButWorthIt!!! Stay Blessed!!!

Remember Feed Your Faith Starve Your Fears. Attitude is everything!!! NotPerfectButWorthIt!!! Stay Blessed!!!

Remember Stop chasing the PROBLEMS in life with complaining, negativity, etc., but chase the PROMISES of God with Love, Faith, Joy, and Peace! Attitude is everything!!! NotPerfectButWorthIt!!! Stay Blessed!!!

Remember Keep your eyes on God-your source of help. Attitude is everything!!!NotPerfectButWorthIt!!! Stay Blessed!!!

Remember Nothing you do today will be a surprise to God! Either you will Re-present him or not! Attitude is everything!!! NotPerfectButWorthIt!!! Stay Blessed!!!

Remember Why are you surprised?!? If you're not attacked; you're not a threat! Attitude is everything!!! NotPerfectButWorthIt!!! Stay Blessed!!!

Remember Don't be selfish with your blessing. Attitude is everything!!! NotPerfectButWorthIt!!! Stay Blessed!!!

Remember you already know it's going to be a good day because your still here to be a part of it. Be thankful!!!

Attitude is everything!!! NotPerfectButWorthIt!!! Stay Blessed!!!

Remember to understand that your path has already been chosen. Just continue to be you in every situation and stay straight. People will try to knock you off that path or pull you from it with different ways. We might stumble but thank God for being a God of second chances and keep moving forward. Attitude is everything!!! NotPerfectButWorthIt!!! Stay Blessed!!!

Remember we're not what people say you are you are what God say we are!!! Attitude is everything!!! NotPerfectButWorthIt!!! Stay Blessed!!!

Remember life really is so simple but people choose to make it difficult. If God is all you have then you have all you need!!! Make someone smile and encourage them today we can all use that in our lives. Attitude is everything!!! NotPerfectButWorthIt!!! Stay Blessed!!!

Remember once we understand that God is bigger than anything we face we will walk with a boldness like no other. Stand for something and allow God to use you. Somebody, somewhere is depending on you to do what God has called you to do!!! Attitude is everything!!! NotPerfectButWorthIt!!! Stay Blessed!!!

Remember It's only by his grace and mercy we are still here today. Please don't take that for granted. It is so easy to get caught up in things where we can forget that. Stand in his greatness and smile in the face of those who challenge you today with negatively!!! Attitude is everything!!! NotPerfectButWorthIt!!! Stay Blessed!!!

Remember don't allow anything to hold you back from growing and going to where God wants you to be. I saw this flower where I go to walk in the morning and it made me think about how did that one flower brake through all that heavy concrete. It hit me that flower was determined to grow and brake through whatever it is trying to hold it back and that's how we need to live. Attitude is everything!!! NotPerfectButWorthIt!!! Stay Blessed!!!

Remember when you take the time in your busy day to stop and think about what God has done for you how can you have a bad day. Don't waste your time being angry about things you can't control it doesn't change anything it's our choice how to handle things!!! Attitude is everything!!! NotPerfectButWorthIt!!! Stay Blessed!!!

Remember the Lord doesn't make mistakes, it's been raining a lot because things need to grow. So just understand that we go through the rain in our life's because God needs something in us to grow. Endure the process and we will come out bigger and stronger than before!!! Attitude is everything!!! NotPerfectButWorthIt!!! Stay Blessed!!!

Remember It's so easy to lose focus with all the things around you. Some things have to go if it's not helping you grow!!!

MJMS &LPM - 458

I looked in the mirror this morning and saw the person that's holding me back and all this time I thought it was somebody else. Make no excuses you have a gift from God use it!!! Attitude is everything!!! NotPerfectButWorthIt!!! Stay Blessed!!!

Remember your yesterday has come and gone, so step out today refresh and new. You have places to go and lives to affect in a positive way. So go be the change in your surroundings!!! Attitude is everything!!! NotPerfectButWorthIt!!! Stay Blessed!!!

Remember life may not always be fair but God is always Faithful. Keep on pushing your closer than you think!!! Attitude is everything!!! NotPerfectButWorthIt!!! Stay Blessed!!!

Remember when you wake up in the morning never forget to take the time to thank God for another day and get your mind right. The enemy starts early and keeps coming all day. If your mindset isn't ready you can lose before you even walk out the door. Lord I pray we set our mind right and stay focused on the prize. Make the enemy stand down Amen!!! Attitude is everything!!! NotPerfectButWorthIt!!! Stay Blessed!!!

Remember keep your fire lit so that you can continue to be a bright light in a dark world. Times are hard and a lot of people are getting out of control, but we don't need to criticize others but pray for others. Prayer really changes things!!! Attitude is everything!!! NotPerfectButWorthIt!!! Stay Blessed!!!

Remember be careful the enemy loves to show you only the moment but not the consequences. So before you act out of character take THAT moment to think positive thoughts. Staying on that topic today because we really need to stay focused and recognize!!! Attitude is everything!!! NotPerfectButWorthIt!!! Stay Blessed!!!

Remember we need to remember the enemy takes no days off, so you can't take no days off depending on God. Even if it seems nothing is going wrong he is plotting and waiting for you to put your guards down. He doesn't want you to depend on God so he acts like he's not around. Renew your mind "EVERYDAY" even if it's only with a thank you Jesus. It will bring you a calm and positive attitude!!! Attitude is everything!!! NotPerfectButWorthIt!!! Stay Blessed!!!

Remember to say thank you Lord for not giving us what our sins deserve. We know we're not perfect but you show us we are worth it every day you allow us to wake up. I found that it's hard to complain while praising your name Lord. Continue to keep us from the hands of the wicked, it's so easy to get caught up in out fast pace lives with the negative that we miss our blessings. Help us stay focus on the positive things. Amen!!! We all deal with things about us that seems to have a hold on us and the only way to break that is to be transparent with God. Asked him to release that thing out of your life and watch him work. Stand on that and believe!!! Attitude is everything!!! NotPerfectButWorthIt!!! Stay Blessed!!!

Remember yes even on a Monday your blessing can come. So stay prepared with an open mind to receive it because it's coming!!! Attitude is everything!!! NotPerfectButWorthIt!!! Stay Blessed!!!

Remember life is never going to stop. We will always have challenges but strong, steady faith will cause us to overcome them all. It's easy said than done but if you do it he will bring you through it. Stand on that and believe!!! Attitude is everything!!! NotPerfectButWorthIt!!! Stay Blessed!!!

Remember we need to learn how to step aside and allow God to fight our battles. Don't get sucked into what people opinions of you are. Remember you don't have to value their opinion in the first place. Just place it in God's hands and he got you. Less stress allows you to be at your best!!! Attitude is everything!!! NotPerfectButWorthIt!!! Stay Blessed!!!

Remember to send out a midday reminder to let this day bless you not stress you. Stay encouraged and keep your joy!!! Attitude is everything!!! NotPerfectButWorthIt!!! Stay Blessed!!!

Remember you can reach out and grab your dream for two reasons. One it's yours and two you believe in yourself. What surprises me is the percentage of people that don't even believe in themselves.God would've gave you the gift if he didn't believe you could do it. It's yours!!! Attitude is everything!!! NotPerfectButWorthIt!!! Stay Blessed!!!

Remember It's not the bad days that get you, it's how you react to a bad day. I really believe it's your choice to let it bring you down or not. You can recover from a bad day and you can stand up strong after a fall. There is an inner strength in us that we need to always tap into. So dig deep and come out strong because you a child of God!!! Attitude is everything!!! NotPerfectButWorthIt!!! Stay Blessed!!!

Remember today as you face obstacles in your life already have the mindset that you won't be stopped. God has a mission for you to complete in life. So keep pushing until that obstacle turns into your path. Being committed is key!!! Attitude is everything!!! NotPerfectButWorthIt!!! Stay Blessed!!!

Remember let's get this new week started out right knowing that God is with you every step of the way. No one can stop his plans for you so you are already winning, even on a Monday. God is that good!!! Attitude is everything!!! NotPerfectButWorthIt!!! Stay Blessed!!!

Remember If I were still trying to please people, I would not be a servant of Christ. Be a God pleaser he is the one that loves you no matter what. His grace and mercy is ever lasting while people is for a moment or a season. Thank you Lord for allowing us another day to be a servant and a light in this dark world!!! Attitude is everything!!! NotPerfectButWorthIt!!! Stay Blessed!!!

Remember welcome Monday in just like you should welcome Friday thankful and with a smile. Why shouldn't we be thankful? God allowed us to be able to get out the bed and move our bodies. As we look forward to this week develop the mindset of victory in everything you do and you will have a successful week!!! Attitude is everything!!! NotPerfectButWorthIt!!! Stay Blessed!!!

Remember that people are going to judge you regardless so be judged by your actions and not your talk. I love the saying I can show you better than I can tell you. Give the naysayers something to watch and let them talk about it and ask you how do you stay positive. Then let them know because God is still God!!! Attitude is everything!!! NotPerfectButWorthIt!!! Stay Blessed!!!

Remember don't carry an ounce of guilt around about your past which includes yesterday because you have been forgiven. We are going to make mistakes because we're not perfect, but we know a perfect God and he says all is forgiven. So release that heavy burden and enjoy life. Smile so much that it will be impossible to see you and not smile. The attitude you carry will change others around attitude. So keep it positive!!! Attitude is everything!!! NotPerfectButWorthIt!!! Stay Blessed!!!

Remember glory be to God for waking us up this morning. Not your clock, not your significant other but God. We have to learn to be thankful for everything even if you think it's a small thing. He loves us so much even when we don't deserve it. Being thank always make your day great because there's nothing to complain about!!! Attitude is everything!!! NotPerfectButWorthIt!!! Stay Blessed!!!

Remember I know sometimes things can really be discouraging and it seems to not have an end, but this too shall pass. Keep the faith that God is working it out!!! Attitude is everything!!! NotPerfectButWorthIt!!! Stay Blessed!!!

Remember living in fear is not living. You have everything you need to do whatever it is you want to do in this world. Even if the odds are stacked against you, you know a God that's bigger than anything stacked against you. It's there for the taking. All your hopes and all your dreams. Have faith and go get it. Welcome back Monday you don't scare me!!! Attitude is everything!!! NotPerfectButWorthIt!!! Stay Blessed!!!

Remember if you choose to stay angry you are allowing the enemy to come through the door. I just dropped off my daughter this morning to school and I was sitting in a very long line when this one person decides to drive pass all of us that was patiently waiting sat in the middle of the street to cut in line one car before me and I was livid. At that moment I allowed the enemy in my head because I wasn't ready to let go the anger. Keep your prayer life alive because we need it every single day. We must choose not to allow him in because he can ready mess up your day before it even get started. Keep it positive!!! Attitude is everything!!! NotPerfectButWorthIt!!! Stay Blessed!!!

Remember if anyone ask you today how did you make it tell them LOUD and PROUD it's because of God's grace and mercy. Enough said!!! Attitude is everything!!! NotPerfectButWorthIt!!! Stay Blessed!!!

Remember have confidence in yourself God didn't make any mistakes with you. He made you strong as you need to be in every situation. Don't allow the enemy to make you feel any less about yourself. He will use people all around you to bring you down but continue to stand strong and claim victory!!! Attitude is everything!!! NotPerfectButWorthIt!!! Stay Blessed!!!

Remember to think what a beautiful morning to be alive and grateful. Just thinking that someone didn't wake up this morning tells us we should be grateful for his Grace. God doesn't need us he wants us. That's what's so amazing to me. That fact that he can use our mess and turn it into a message. Your story is already written so just stay in your lane for a beautiful ending for his glory!!! Attitude is everything!!! NotPerfectButWorthIt!!! Stay Blessed!!!

Remember Monday's are hard to adapt to for some so learning to maintain a Monday is key. Attitude is everything!!! NotPerfectButWorthIt!!! Stay Blessed!!!

Remember you can have peace in this hateful world, just don't let your feelings get in the way of your Faith!!! Attitude is everything!!! NotPerfectButWorthIt!!! Stay Blessed!!!

Remember you can't fight this battle called life in your own strength, but the good news is that God will fight your battles. Just lean on him and keep your faith. Now go into your weekend with absolutely no worries!!! Attitude is everything!!! NotPerfectButWorthIt!!! Stay Blessed!!!

Remember stop choosing on what day you need God because we need him EVERY single day. The enemy doesn't take one day off not one and if it feels like your coasting it's because he's waiting and doesn't want you to depend on God. Make sure you keep your focus!!! Attitude is everything!!! NotPerfectButWorthIt!!! Stay Blessed!!!

Remember to try and get a hold on your emotions. You can feel a certain way but don't act on it. It only takes a few seconds to change your whole attitude which changes your whole day. Life is not fair but God is just, He takes wrong things and make them right. Stand and believe that!!! Attitude is everything!!! NotPerfectButWorthIt!!! Stay Blessed!!!

Remember that a bad attitude brings nothing but negativity. Sometimes I wonder how some people can wake up with a bad attitude instead of being thankful to see another day. They already claimed defeat for their day. Make the decision to be thankful and claim victory in Jesus name for your day!!! Attitude is everything!!! NotPerfectButWorthIt!!! Stay Blessed!!!

Remember we have to check our attitudes some times and remember that our story is already written from beginning to the end. So if your day is not going so great in the way you want it check your attitude. How we react will make it better or worse!!! Attitude is everything!!! NotPerfectButWorthIt!!! Stay Blessed!!!

Remember you don't need people to hold your hand when you understand that God got you!!! Attitude is everything!!! NotPerfectButWorthIt!!! Stay Blessed!!!

Remember it's hard to be DOWN when you're UP praising his name. Now go make the enemy mad because he can't have you or your peace!!! Attitude is everything!!! NotPerfectButWorthIt!!! Stay Blessed!!!

Remember Monday is back and so are we. Grateful and ready for what comes our way because at the end of the day we stay winning because God is on our side. Stand on and believe that!!! Attitude is everything!!! NotPerfectButWorthIt!!! Stay Blessed!!!

Remember get it in your mind "Not Today or Any Day" will anyone take your Joy!!! Stand on and Believe that!!! Attitude is everything!!! NotPerfectButWorthIt!!! Stay Blessed!!!

Remember being patient is a process in itself that no one likes, but remember to renew your mind every day and keep an attitude that help you stay in the moment. Focus only on the positive and not the negative. God got you!!! Attitude is everything!!! NotPerfectButWorthIt!!! Stay Blessed!!!

Remember we can't allow just anybody to speak into our lives, it can have such a negative effect. Keep your circle tight and filled with love and positivity!!! Attitude is everything!!! NotPerfectButWorthIt!!! Stay Blessed!!!

Remember we live in a fast past world so don't forget to slow down and take the time to encourage someone. You never know who needs a nice smile or word in their life!!! Make somebody's day!!! Attitude is everything!!! NotPerfectButWorthIt!!! Stay Blessed!!!

Remember always keep this in mind, a new day means a new chance. If yesterday wasn't your day maybe it's today. Just continue to have faith and know that you are loved no matter your situation. Claim your victory!!! Attitude is everything!!! NotPerfectButWorthIt!!! Stay Blessed!!!

Remember no one can stop what God has for you, act like it and take what's yours. God has plans for each and every one of us. No need to worry about someone else plan just focus on what he has for you and stay in your lane and keep winning. Attitude is everything!!! NotPerfectButWorthIt!!! Stay Blessed!!!

Remember happy Monday to you. I know a lot of people that don't like Monday because it's the start of a new work week, but what if you didn't wake up on Monday? What if you didn't have a job on Monday? Never stop being grateful. Good things can happen on Monday; we just need to change our mindset!!! Attitude is everything!!! NotPerfectButWorthIt!!! Stay Blessed!!!

Remember a positive attitude can change the atmosphere in every room you walk into. Remember you only get one chance for a first impression. No one wants to be around a negative person unless they too are a negative person. Keep your smile even if it hurts because today will be a good day!!! Attitude is everything!!! NotPerfectButWorthIt!!! Stay Blessed!!!

Remember if we treated everyday like Friday just imagine what kind of attitude we would have every day and if we had the attitude of Christ just imagine how the world can change. Just something to think about!!! Attitude is everything!!! NotPerfectButWorthIt!!! Stay Blessed!!!

Remember stop denying yourself happiness by walking around with a bad attitude. Do you know some people wake up mad and frustrated? It automatically ruins their day. Start your day out by thanking God for one more day and being grateful. You won't have time to have a bad attitude. Friendly advice stay away from the mad faces. Attitude is everything!!! NotPerfectButWorthIt!!! Stay Blessed!!!

Remember when I look at a temporary no parking sign it reminds me that problems are just temporary so don't park in the problem. Just keep on moving forward and you will make it through. Your attitude is everything continue to stay positive!!! Attitude is everything!!! NotPerfectButWorthIt!!! Stay Blessed!!!

Remember do you know who you are? Do you understand you are a child of the most high? So why sit around worrying and complaining when God got you, but you have to do your part. Make time or make excuses. Keep your faith in him!!! Attitude is everything!!! NotPerfectButWorthIt!!! Stay Blessed!!!

Remember the process was never created to break you but it is in place to prepare you and get you ready for what you face. Don't lose sight of or forfeit the promise simply because you get a little uncomfortable during the process. The process can get uncomfortable sometimes it feels unbearable but trust God and you can endure. He really has plans for you so get ready!!! Attitude is everything!!! NotPerfectButWorthIt!!! Stay Blessed!!!

Remember to make good use of your time. Don't waste it watching and wondering what other people are doing, do you. God has different plans for everyone so get a hold on your plan and run with it. I get it our flesh sometimes think why them, but just think for a moment why me? It's because he loves us all even though we were and sometimes still are a mess. (Again thanking you for Grace and Mercy) So stay in your lane your time is coming. Just continue to focus and be discipline!!! Attitude is everything!!! NotPerfectButWorthIt!!! Stay Blessed!!!

Remember praise his name just because!!! I know time flies but take time to praise him. For we serve a great God that loves us through it all. The good the bad and the ugly. We can't say that for people. They will abandon ship in a heartbeat but God will hold you down no matter what. So we are blessed more than we know. Thank you lord for loving a mess like me!!! Attitude is everything!!! NotPerfectButWorthIt!!! Stay Blessed!!!

Remember regardless of what you hear God has the final say. Just a reminder that our God is bigger than whatever you facing or whatever you will face in life. Stand on and believe that!!! Attitude is everything!!! NotPerfectButWorthIt!!! Stay Blessed!!!

Remember to take on this Monday morning with the same attitude we take on Friday morning. Excited and grateful and you can't lose. Bad days can't phase you with the attitude of gratefulness!!! Attitude is everything!!! NotPerfectButWorthIt!!! Stay Blessed!!!

Remember a positive person doesn't fit in a negative situation. So be careful of your surroundings. You can't hang or just let anyone speak into your life. Everyone is not always for you or on your side. Again your trust is in God so stay focused and push forward through your roadblocks because some of those roadblocks are closer than think. Knowing is the easy part facing reality is the challenge!!! Attitude is everything!!! NotPerfectButWorthIt!!! Stay Blessed!!!

Remember where you're going is more important than where you've been. Don't let your past hold back your future!!! Attitude is everything!!! NotPerfectButWorthIt!!! Stay Blessed!!!

Remember if you only have 5 steps left in you, go 10 more just in case you have any doubters. God gives us the strength to keep going even when we don't feel like it or think we can!!! Attitude is everything!!! NotPerfectButWorthIt!!! Stay Blessed!!!

Remember today let's just come together and agree that today will be a great day. No one will be able to ruin your day or take away your joy. Just stand on and believe that. Enjoy your great day!!! Attitude is everything!!! NotPerfectButWorthIt!!! Stay Blessed!!!

Remember Thank God he loves us in our imperfections. We need him each and every day. So never take for granted the seed that was planted!!! Attitude is everything!!! NotPerfectButWorthIt!!! Stay Blessed!!!

Remember God's word is sometimes like Medicine it doesn't always seem good, but it's good for you! Next time you get it, receive it, and watch it work in you!!! Attitude is everything!!! NotPerfectButWorthIt!!! Stay Blessed!!!

Remember yesterday can make you a better person if you use it wisely. Just take all the positive things that you've learned and Attitude is everything!!! NotPerfectButWorthIt!!! Stay Blessed!!!

Remember many times the answer for us in our struggles is not to change the world around us but to change the world within us. It starts from the inside!!! Attitude is everything!!! NotPerfectButWorthIt!!! Stay Blessed!!!

Remember you can't appreciate freedom unless you've been bound before. So as you go through things just know that this too shall pass and there is freedom on the other of a storm. Trust that God is working it out for your good!!! Attitude is everything!!! NotPerfectButWorthIt!!! Stay Blessed!!!

Remember continue to trust in God's plan for you, he will never fail you!!! Attitude is everything!!! NotPerfectButWorthIt!!! Stay Blessed!!!

Remember your attitude can affect yours and somebody's else's day in a good or a bad way, so keep it positive!!! Attitude is everything!!! NotPerfectButWorthIt!!! Stay Blessed!!!

Remember whoever you come in contact with today send them off with a word of encouragement, because you never know who needs it or what it can do for someone's life!!! Attitude is everything!!! NotPerfectButWorthIt!!! Stay Blessed!!!

Remember to understand what makes God smile, You, so continue to give him a reason to smile down on you!!! Attitude is everything!!! NotPerfectButWorthIt!!! Stay Blessed!!!

Remember they might think you stand alone but when you're in the will of God, NOTHING can stand in the way of your purpose!!! Attitude is everything!!! NotPerfectButWorthIt!!! Stay Blessed!!!

Remember, I know it's Monday and we are right back at work but last time I checked waking up on Monday and having a job is a blessing. So be thankful and make somebody else day with a smile and a word of encouragement!!! Attitude is everything!!! NotPerfectButWorthIt!!! Stay Blessed!!!

Remember to learn how to endure the process and how to embrace all the wonderful blessings God has in store for your future. God wants to have a relationship with us and nothing but the best for us. Father I pray right now for all of us continue to grow in you and have a better relationship with you. I pray that we all realize there is a gift that you gave in each and every one of us and we reach full potential using this gift. I also just ask that you to continue to keep us all covered in Jesus wonderful and powerful name. Amen!!! Attitude is everything!!! NotPerfectButWorthIt!!! Stay Blessed!!!

Remember the answer for everything is trust God in anything. Stand on and believe that!!! Attitude is everything!!! NotPerfectButWorthIt!!! Stay Blessed!!!

Remember that God's unfailing love is priceless, so show some of that love to someone today and watch how it's affect is priceless!!! Attitude is everything!!! NotPerfectButWorthIt!!! Stay Blessed!!!

Remember don't compromise and accept a poor substitute for the greatness that God has coming for you.
If we dare to believe God's word, we can have light in the middle of a dark world!!! Attitude is everything!!! NotPerfectButWorthIt!!! Stay Blessed!!!

Remember that some say sky is the limit, but why stop there when God created the sky? Which means with God there is no limit. So be limitless in your connection with God!!! Attitude is everything!!! NotPerfectButWorthIt!!! Stay Blessed!!!

Remember not to lose your way because of somebody else's attitude. Don't allow their bad day become yours. Instead let your positive attitude become theirs and change their day!!! Attitude is everything!!! NotPerfectButWorthIt!!! Stay Blessed!!!

Remember it's not always easy to do the right thing, but it's the right thing to do. We already know that we will be put to the test daily, so we have the advantage to be prepared. So seek God for your peace and he will provide your mind with ease!!! Attitude is everything!!! NotPerfectButWorthIt!!! Stay Blessed!!!

Remember if God isn't in control, things will be out of control!!! Just keep a positive attitude in your daily life and you can make it. Now go make this day one of the best days in your life!!! Attitude is everything!!! NotPerfectButWorthIt!!! Stay Blessed!!!

Remember when God acts on our behalf, he can turn any situation around in a heartbeat. So give your worries to him and keep your mind at peace!!! Attitude is everything!!! NotPerfectButWorthIt!!! Stay Blessed!!!

Remember sometimes your storm may feel bigger than someone else's storm and it might be, but know that God is bigger than any storm. God is always there for you and love you. Stand on and believe that!!! Attitude is everything!!! NotPerfectButWorthIt!!! Stay Blessed!!!

Remember decide today that you are more than a conqueror, you are blessed beyond measure regardless of any situation that's going on, God got you. He woke you up this morning to do something special. Walk like it, talk like it and allow your faith to remove your fears. Stand on and believe that!!!

Attitude is everything!!! NotPerfectButWorthIt!!! Stay Blessed!!!

Remember when it's Monday there are a lot of Monday haters, so don't entertain negative thoughts or negative people it can weigh you down for the rest of your day. Changing your thinking will lighten your load!!! Attitude is everything!!! NotPerfectButWorthIt!!! Stay Blessed!!!

I was just looking out my window watching how it's raining outside but it's shining inside. Which made me think about some people that are shining outside but raining inside. In other words, you never know what people are going through from the look of things so always treat people they way you want to be treated!!! Attitude is everything!!! NotPerfectButWorthIt!!! Stay Blessed!!!

Remember don't stress yourself out in life trying to make something happen that only God can make happen. Lean on him and not your own understanding. All you need to understand is he got you!!! Attitude is everything!!! NotPerfectButWorthIt!!! Stay Blessed!!!

Remember until you treat your vision and dream like it's yours it will stay on hold. Commit yourself to it and never abandon your mission, keep pushing until it happens because God gave it to you!!! Attitude is everything!!! NotPerfectButWorthIt!!! Stay Blessed!!!

Remember to develop patience because the process can be slow but the amazing thing is, you will have a WOW moment because God will show up and show out for you every time. He loves us that much!!! Attitude is everything!!! NotPerfectButWorthIt!!! Stay Blessed!!!

Remember when the enemy reminds you of all your failures, thank him for reminding you because now you can be extra grateful for God's forgiveness!!! Attitude is everything!!! NotPerfectButWorthIt!!! Stay Blessed!!!

Remember we don't have to be defeated by the attitudes of the world. God has given us a way to have hope and comfort, as we go into the new week claim victory every day!!! Attitude is everything!!! NotPerfectButWorthIt!!! Stay Blessed!!!

Remember things don't always go your way and things change all the time, but God's word remains the same. So stand on it and believe he will work it out!!! Attitude is everything!!! NotPerfectButWorthIt!!! Stay Blessed!!!

Remember complaining changes nothing but faith and prayer changes everything.Trust God in any storm to pull you through!!! Attitude is everything!!! NotPerfectButWorthIt!!! Stay Blessed!!!

Remember not to give up on ourselves? God refuses to give up on us. Yes, we make mistakes but thank God for his mercy and grace. Keep going and keep growing!!! Attitude is everything!!! NotPerfectButWorthIt!!! Stay Blessed!!!

Remember as you go into a new week just continue to feed yourself positive thoughts and negative thoughts will have no room in your mind!!! Attitude is everything!!! NotPerfectButWorthIt!!! Stay Blessed!!!

Remember we have more power and strength than we realize, we just need to release the power that God instilled in us. We can control our emotions and feelings when someone do us wrong. We can say no to those wicked thoughts. We can control our tongue, with faith and knowing that God is working behind the scenes!!! Attitude is everything!!! NotPerfectButWorthIt!!! Stay Blessed!!!

Remember the enemy can't stop us so he tries to get us to quit because he knows if we keep going we will win. Be a winner not a quitter. Have patience and continue to move forward. You will reap what you sow!!! Attitude is everything!!! NotPerfectButWorthIt!!! Stay Blessed!!!

Remember think about the possibilities not the problems. If we can take time for pity parties, we can take time to celebrate our victories. What we focus on is what we magnify. So choose to focus on the victories!!! Attitude is everything!!! NotPerfectButWorthIt!!! Stay Blessed!!!

Remember to keep your light shining. There will be dark moments in life but never let it dim your light. There is a King in you!!! Attitude is everything!!! NotPerfectButWorthIt!!! Stay Blessed!!!

Remember people don't determine your destiny, God determines your destiny. I know we always say you have to know somebody that know somebody, but when we know the name above all names that's all we need to know. If we just have faith and believe. God knows all the somebodies that can put us in the place we need to be!!! Attitude is everything!!! NotPerfectButWorthIt!!! Stay Blessed!!!

Remember when you go through things look at it as an opportunity for God to be glorified because you know he always works it out!!!
Attitude is everything!!! NotPerfectButWorthIt!!! Stay Blessed!!!

Remember you don't have to accept negativity in your life. People that are joy killers, those that don't want or to see you grow. The math is easy 3 positive people in your life adds more value to your life than 5 negative people. Take your 3 and change the world!!! Attitude is everything!!! NotPerfectButWorthIt!!! Stay Blessed!!!

Remember rejection is a sign that God has something better for you, so don't be bitter be better. If you decide to stop then you lose. Winners continue to move forward!!! Attitude is everything!!! NotPerfectButWorthIt!!! Stay Blessed!!!

Remember a new year means nothing without a new mind set. Positive thinking is our mission and it's what a lot of us is missing. We were created to do big things in life. So let go of anything negative because it will only weigh you down!!! Attitude is everything!!! NotPerfectButWorthIt!!! Stay Blessed!!!

Remember we may not stick with God all the time in our decision making but he always stick with us and thank God for his mercy and grace because a lot of our decisions are from emotions. Seek him first!!! Attitude is everything!!! NotPerfectButWorthIt!!! Stay Blessed!!!

Remember as long as God protects and watches over us in heaven, there is no one on earth who can break us. There is safety in him!!! Always keep your joy. Attitude is everything!!! NotPerfectButWorthIt!!! Stay Blessed!!!

Remember we are everything we are because God love us. Show his love back and be a blessing in someone's life!!! Attitude is everything!!! NotPerfectButWorthIt!!! Stay Blessed!!!

Remember to take control of your week starting today. It's not just another day, it's another opportunity. So don't be limited to what God wants to do in your life!!! Attitude is everything!!! NotPerfectButWorthIt!!! Stay Blessed!!!

Remember the task ahead of you is never great as the power behind you!!! Be strong in the Lord, and in his mighty power!!! Attitude is everything!!! NotPerfectButWorthIt!!! Stay Blessed!!!

Remember to always push yourself to the limit and then keep going forward. No one wants it more than you do so no one will push harder for you than you. You're stronger than you think. If God is for us WHO can be against us? Attitude is everything!!! NotPerfectButWorthIt!!! Stay Blessed!!!

Remember to think outside the box because we can do all things through Christ who strengthens us. So who can stop us for going after anything??? He is our foundation and that makes us strong!!! Attitude is everything!!! NotPerfectButWorthIt!!! Stay Blessed!!!

Remember there's a process for everything. Go through it because the process is what makes you. God is always working it out for your good!!! Attitude is everything!!! NotPerfectButWorthIt!!! Stay Blessed!!!

Remember not to feel that you must meet a certain standard to feel good about yourself. God love you for who you are and so should you!!! Attitude is everything!!! NotPerfectButWorthIt!!! Stay Blessed!!!

Remember to start every day out with a Grateful heart and God is your source not man. Attitude is everything!!! NotPerfectButWorthIt!!! Stay Blessed!!!

Remember if you want different you have to be different.

Staying the same is like going backwards, always look to improve and keep pushing forward past all the negative things and people that wants to hold you back from your purpose!!! Attitude is everything!!! NotPerfectButWorthIt!!! Stay Blessed!!!

Remember never RSVP to a pity party. Attitude is everything!!! NotPerfectButWorthIt!!! Stay Blessed!!!

Remember you can always pull one positive out of a negative and that is it could have been worse. Life is always going to bring things your way but it's how you handle it. God is bigger!!! Attitude is everything!!! NotPerfectButWorthIt!!! Stay Blessed!!!

Remember to start where you are, use what you have, do what you can to affectively make a change for the better!!! Attitude is everything!!! NotPerfectButWorthIt!!! Stay Blessed!!!

Remember God's purpose requires our participation. His blessings follow Faith, Obedience and Perseverance. Life is not what happens to us, it's what we make happen. So let's do our part and make it happen!!! Attitude is everything!!! NotPerfectButWorthIt!!! Stay Blessed!!!

Remember to trust God with your yes and make sure you talk to him every day, because he loves to hear your voice!!! Attitude is everything!!! NotPerfectButWorthIt!!! Stay Blessed!!!

Remember Monday is just another day like any other day, a BLESSED one because we're still here to enjoy it. So don't take it for granted!!! Attitude is everything!!! NotPerfectButWorthIt!!! Stay Blessed!!!

Remember if you don't think God is blessing you just think about this your heart is still beating!!! Attitude is everything!!! NotPerfectButWorthIt!!! Stay Blessed!!!

Remember to see your true worth through God's eyes and not people. As long God is pleased that's all that matters!!! Attitude is everything!!! NotPerfectButWorthIt!!! Stay Blessed!!!

Remember to think before you speak. Don't allow anger to get the best of you. If you are going through something keep in mind that this too shall pass and God will bring you through it. Keep your faith and keep it positive!!! Attitude is everything!!! NotPerfectButWorthIt!!! Stay Blessed!!!

Remember God doesn't just want you to exist he wants you to live!!! So enjoy living and keep a positive mindset set!!! Attitude is everything!!! NotPerfectButWorthIt!!! Stay Blessed!!!

Remember quality over quantity, it doesn't matter how many friends you have it's about having the right friends.
The ones that has your best interest and wants you to excel. Care's about your well-being. So who's better to be friends with than Christ? Who do you know that would make

that sacrifice for us? No relationship like it!!! Attitude is everything!!! NotPerfectButWorthIt!!! Stay Blessed!!!

Remember a successful day is up to you. An attitude of gratefulness will bring you that success because absolutely no one can take your happiness because you are too grateful for life!!! Attitude is everything!!! NotPerfectButWorthIt!!! Stay Blessed!!!

Remember not to wait on a feeling to motivate you, do it by faith. Trust God will make it happen. The Bible says that when you pray in faith, believe it and you will receive it. Are we praying just to pray or praying in faith. Attitude is everything!!! NotPerfectButWorthIt!!! Stay Blessed!!!

Remember that it is a choice when you wake up in the morning to go forward with a positive attitude or a negative attitude. So choose wisely because it will make the difference in your day. So say happy new day I'm ready!!! Attitude is everything!!! NotPerfectButWorthIt!!! Stay Blessed!!!

Remember we all need the grace of God because we are only flesh and bones, so we're not perfect, but at the same time it's not an excuse or reason to be negative or mean to people. It's all about positively and love!!! Attitude is everything!!! NotPerfectButWorthIt!!! Stay Blessed!!!

Remember don't throw away your confidence. Increase it by keeping the love in the goodness of God in your heart and in your mouth. You are stronger than you know!!! Attitude is everything!!! NotPerfectButWorthIt!!! Stay Blessed!!!

Remember caring can touch where words can't reach. Show some love every opportunity you get just like God shows us love every day!!! Attitude is everything!!! NotPerfectButWorthIt!!! Stay Blessed!!!

Remember there's a lot of people going through things in their life that's controllable and not controllable, but the good news is we don't have to only rely on ourselves. We have a God that can control what we can't control!!! Attitude is everything!!! NotPerfectButWorthIt!!! Stay Blessed!!!

Remember God has an assignment for us to complete, so be prepared for the enemy to attack because your assignment is to change things for the better. So stand strong in the Lord!!! Attitude is everything!!! NotPerfectButWorthIt!!! Stay Blessed!!!

Remember a grateful heart overcomes all our want's. God supplies all our needs. So we straight!!! Attitude is everything!!! NotPerfectButWorthIt!!! Stay Blessed!!!

Remember trying to skip a step of the process will not speed it up it will actually slow it up. Trust and believe God is working his part out. We just need to work ours out!!! Attitude is everything!!! NotPerfectButWorthIt!!! Stay Blessed!!!

Empowerment

Remember a new day brings new trails but continue to keep your patience because patience develops strength of character in us and helps us trust God more each time we use it until finally our hope and faith are strong and steady!!! Attitude is everything!!! NotPerfectButWorthIt!!! Stay Blessed!!!

Remember that God has a plan for you and only you, so stay on course and don't lose focus. As things get rough just endure because you will make it through. Stand on and believe that!!! Attitude is everything!!! NotPerfectButWorthIt!!! Stay Blessed!!!

Remember as we start this busy week of run, run, run, go, go, go, make sure you take time out thank God for another day. Never get too busy for that. We are going through our day's way to fast and way too much without God in it. We need to stay connected to the source to stay on course!!! Attitude is everything!!! NotPerfectButWorthIt!!! Stay Blessed!!!

Remember keep your mind focused on the things you need to stay focused on. The enemy loves to play with your mind and have you upset about things you really don't care or need to concern yourself about. It's a tough battle but you can win. Continue to remind yourself through all things yes through all things you can do anything through Christ who gives you strength!!! Attitude is everything!!! NotPerfectButWorthIt!!! Stay Blessed!!!

Remember to take time out today and say a prayer for someone. Prayer can change things around. Give someone an encouraging word you never know how much they need it and how much it helps. Inspire someone to focus on their goals because it's so easy to lose focus. In other words Think Positive, Speak Positive and Live Positive!!! Attitude is everything!!! NotPerfectButWorthIt!!! Stay Blessed!!!

Remember to stop focusing on our problems and focus on the promise. The promises of God can be right in front of, yet we are so focused on the problem, that we do not even see the promises. When you are seeing right, your life will accelerate!!! Attitude is everything!!! NotPerfectButWorthIt!!! Stay Blessed!!!

Remember instead of saying why me God, it's got to be a better way. Say thanks be to God. We have been blessed more than we know or can imagine. Attitude is everything!!! NotPerfectButWorthIt!!! Stay Blessed!!!

Remember to face this new week with confidence. A confident person is not afraid of change, it only means God is at work for your good!!! Attitude is everything!!! NotPerfectButWorthIt!!! Stay Blessed!!!

Remember quitting is the easy route, learn to press though all that might be taking place in your life. You will see that God has equipped us with everything we need to be strong. Stand on and believe that!!! Attitude is everything!!! NotPerfectButWorthIt!!! Stay Blessed!!!

Remember NOTHING INTIMIDATES GOD!!! Attitude is everything!!! NotPerfectButWorthIt!!! Stay Blessed!!!

Remember you might feel fear, but you don't have to succumb to it. It's only a feeling. God wants us to be Bold and Confident. Know who you are in Christ!!! Attitude is everything!!! NotPerfectButWorthIt!!! Stay Blessed!!!

Remember the power you have behind you is bigger and stronger than anything you will face in life. Stay prayed up and keep your faith!!! Attitude is everything!!! NotPerfectButWorthIt!!! Stay Blessed!!!

Remember always believe in yourself. Have confidence when you step out after your goals and dreams. With Christ all things are possible. There will be roadblocks and trails in your way but they will make you strong. So keep your faith and all will work out for the good!!! Attitude is everything!!! NotPerfectButWorthIt!!! Stay Blessed!!!

Remember to be strong, become impossible to break. People will try you each and every day. Know who the real enemy is so that you can fight the right way in prayer!!! Attitude is everything!!! NotPerfectButWorthIt!!! Stay Blessed!!!

Remember that we should try and make a positive impact on someone each and every day with being positive ourselves!!! Attitude is everything!!! NotPerfectButWorthIt!!! Stay Blessed!!!

Remember we're more than conquerors through Christ who gives us strength!!! So never stop going after what you want. Attitude is everything!!! NotPerfectButWorthIt!!! Stay Blessed!!!

Remember don't listen to the naysayers the joy stealers, we are not average because we are made in his image. We can do all things through Christ who strengthen us. Haters will come because they see something special in us. Take time to see it yourself and keep pushing towards your destiny!!! Attitude is everything!!! NotPerfectButWorthIt!!! Stay Blessed!!!

Remember behind a smile can be heart break. You just never know what's going on in people's lives. The problems they could be having. True joy is in Christ, so allow him in your life because he wants a relationship with us. It only takes a YES!!! Attitude is everything!!! NotPerfectButWorthIt!!! Stay Blessed!!!

Remember the one who falls and gets up is so much stronger than the one who never fell. So it's ok to fall but you must get up and continue to move forward!!! Attitude is everything!!! NotPerfectButWorthIt!!! Stay Blessed!!!

Remember not to allow the fear of failure stop you. There is greatness in each and every one on us. Today can be your day. Just stay focused and believe!!! Attitude is everything!!! NotPerfectButWorthIt!!! Stay Blessed!!!

Remember every day may not be good, but there is something good in every day. Stay grateful. Attitude is everything!!! NotPerfectButWorthIt!!! Stay Blessed!!!

Remember the situation you're in doesn't mean it's a permanent condition. Just like it's a new week, it can be a new condition. We are stronger than we think and when we learn not the rely on man but rely on God. That's when you will see the difference. Attitude is everything!!! NotPerfectButWorthIt!!! Stay Blessed!!!

Remember to claim your victories in this new week. You have the power to change things with your attitude and how you carry yourself!!! Attitude is everything!!! NotPerfectButWorthIt!!! Stay Blessed!!!

Remember the only time you should have your head down is when you're praying. God made us more than conquerors, so when things happen will still can keep our head up and press forward!!! Attitude is everything!!! NotPerfectButWorthIt!!! Stay Blessed!!!

About The Author

Marlon Marshall is the co-founder of BRAVE 458, a community based initiative whose focus is providing outreach services to people in need. Though a native of Washington, DC, his family relocated to the Alexandria, VA area; later graduating from the Fairfax County Public School system. With a passion for film, in September 2011, Marlon enrolled in the University of Boston majoring in Film/Digital Programming, and graduated June 2013 with a degree in his major. In his spare time, he enjoys mentoring the youth by giving back in volunteering/coaching for Fairfax County Basketball Youth Leagues, as well as, High School Basketball for both Varsity and Junior Varsity Boys Teams, in both Fairfax and Prince William Counties. Marlon has over 16 years in Telecommunications and outreach through Brave458 in the past years. Marlon is currently employed at a Prince William High School where he is fortune to pour into the children with differening abilities. He currently resides in Woodbridge, VA with his wife Lisa, and their children Marlon, Jr, McKenzye. His daughter Brierra and her family reside in the local DMV area.

Lisa Marshall is the co-founder of BRAVE458, a community based initiative whose focus is providing outreach services to people in need. She was born and raised in Washington, DC, attending DC Public Schools. Upon graduation from high school, Lisa attended and graduated from the University of the District of Columbia where she obtained a Bachelors of Liberal Arts Degree in Journalism (Print Media) in May 1992. In addition to BRAVE458, Lisa has been employed for over 30 years in the Federal Government. Lisa is especially passionate about "women" issues; and the importance of their whole wellness. She currently resides in Woodbridge, VA with her husband Marlon and their children Marlon, Jr and McKenzye. Her daughter Brierra and her family reside in the local DMV area.

Printed in the United States
By Bookmasters